The Monkey Wars

The Monkey Wars

POEMS BY

BRUCE WEIGL

The University of Georgia Press
Athens

© 1985 by Bruce Weigl
Published by the University of Georgia Press
Athens, Georgia 30602

All rights reserved
Set in 10 on 13 Linotron 202 Palatino

The paper in this book meets the guidelines for
permanence and durability of the Committee on
Production Guidelines for Book Longevity of the
Council on Library Resources.

Printed in the United States of America

5 4 3 2

Library of Congress Cataloging in Publication Data

Weigl, Bruce, 1949–
    The monkey wars.

    I. Title.
PS3573.E3835M6   1985   811'.54   84-8755
ISBN 0-8203-0740-8 (alk. paper)
ISBN 0-8203-0741-6 (pbk.: alk. paper)

The publication of this book is supported by a grant from
the National Endowment for the Arts, a federal agency.

FOR CHERYL FLOWERS

Acknowledgments

The author and the publisher gratefully acknowledge the following publications in which these poems first appeared.

Black Warrior Review: "Girl at the Chu Lai Laundry"
Cimarron Review: "The Town Inside," "Limits of Departure," "Catch," and "Hotel Florence"
Field: "A Childhood," "On the Wing" (as "Dorothy Wordsworth"), "1955," and "Killing Chickens"
Missouri Review: "Mercy"
New England Review: "The Streets," "Temple near Quang Tri, Not on the Map," "Homage to Elvis, Homage to the Fathers," and "For the Wife Beater's Wife"
Poetry Now: "The Last Lie"
Quarry West: "Letter to X." and "Small Song for Andrew"
Quarterly West: "Flight" and "Burning Shit at An Khe"
Tar River Poetry: "Surrounding Blues on the Way Down"
Tendril: "Debris," "Song for the Lost Private," "Weeds Among the Garlic," and "The Artificial Waterfall and Woods Scene Clock"
Triquarterly Review: "Song of Napalm," "Hope," "Song for a Lost First Cousin," "Sun," "Elegy for A.," "Regret for the Mourning Doves Who Failed to Mate," "Noise," "Amnesia," and "Snowy Egret"

"Temple near Quang Tri, Not on the Map" also appeared in *Pushcart V* (1980). "Song of Napalm" and "The Last Lie" appeared in *Mother Jones.*

Contents

Amnesia

If there was a world more disturbing than this
Where black clouds bowed down and swallowed you whole
And overgrown tropical plants
Rotted, effervescent in the muggy twilight and monkeys
Screamed something
That came to sound like words to each other
Across the triple-canopy jungle you shared,
You don't remember it.

You tell yourself no and cry a thousand days.
You imagine the crows calling autumn into place
Are your brothers and you could
If only the strength and will were there
Fly up to them to be black
And useful to the wind.

Girl at the Chu Lai Laundry

All this time I had forgotten.
My miserable platoon was moving out
One day in the war and I had my clothes in the laundry.
I ran the two dirt miles,
Convoy already forming behind me. I hit
The block of small hooches and saw her
Twist out the black rope of her hair in the sun.
She did not look up at me,
Not even when I called to her for my clothes.
She said I couldn't have them,
They were wet . . .

Who would've thought the world stops
Turning in the war, the tropical heat like hate
And your platoon moves out without you,
Your wet clothes piled
At the feet of the girl at the laundry,
Beautiful with her facts.

Debris

Beyond the few brave bathers
On the first cold day
We rummaged through the kelp
For bones and shells and driftwood—
Signals from a distant shore.
You cringed when I dug up the rotten gull carcass
And talked me out of the wings
Still laced with flesh.

Boiled in bleach
The skull was beautiful.
I hinged the beak with wire
So it opened to the breadth
Of perch and small bass.
It smelled like a fish wind
And took me back to the cold
Morning I ripped a wild sudden shot
At another gull circling high above the dump
I hunted for rats and birds or anything
To get my fill of blood.

When the gull fell, the air
Dizzy with feathers went cold
And the cold drove through my spine like a nail
So I shot again, and twice more
To stop the wings from flapping in the garbage.
I didn't know how easily I could bring it down,
How hard to finally kill it.
I felt the gull fly up into my chest,
Take my breath

But all these years I've kept it from myself
Until this morning a little razor
Of light streaked
Through the bare trees.

A Childhood

I'm not a superstitious man.
I won't love the ground they'll put me in
But I watched the light fill the city
As the sun went down
And the crackling signs and fronts of buildings,
The rows of lamps
Lit up
In the rhythm we called
First lights . . .
I can't remember what the radio said,
I can't recall the conversations
Of family, the loud voices
Passed across the table as bread.
They shouted, they screamed
And I did not listen
And what is left is not blessed,
Only the one season of family I remember—
The way the world is sometimes
Not inside us,
The way we turn around like children
And it is gone, and for once
It is enough to know
The wrong way of things.

The Town Inside

I come back to where I can't let go anymore:
The house set back in the shade of the palmetto
Is not mine
And though I stand across the street
Trying to call back the gray corner room
I shared too long with my sister,
I see only what is here:
A black-haired girl I don't know
Sweeping out an arch of dust from the porch,
The light dappling her face.
But something's wrong, she sweeps too hard,
She bends the sticks of the broom
Until the dust is gone and the arch
Becomes a short, jerking line
Of what I'm sure is anger.
So little room there is in passing
To connect,
As if I could open my life from across the street
To this house of strangers and their trouble.
And so much love it takes
To make the care well up inside us—
Wrapping us into one richer life . . .
But the words won't work and the girl
Sweeping for all the wrong reasons
Is blurred in the heat
Or in the waste of what I don't understand
Because I can't stop watching her,
I can't rise
Or go down.

Song for a Lost First Cousin

You played Bach for your lover
Whom I heard in the background
Laugh when you whispered it was family calling.
At both ends it rained and your voice
Strained through the wire
So cold and unfamiliar
I couldn't tell you I remembered how we'd stripped:
Beautiful boys in the shower at the public beach,
The skin where your suit had been so white
It burns my eyes to remember.
Yet we let go now so carelessly
The minutes break open as eggs
And when I try to speak
I only stutter, only lie.

Long after our connection's broken
And you've turned away from me
I still hold the phone to my ear
As if through the buzzing, static pain
Your voice will break and you will recall
Those mornings and that confusion of love
Between the frightened boys we were
Shivering, perched on the pier's edge,
Oh can't you see us, our arms
Wrapped around each other
Inside the white cocoon of the towel.
But the line's gone dead and we can't
Connect to touch and only the chill
Off the water comes as the rain stops

And whitecaps rise and disappear as fish
And gulls dip their beaks
Into the lake and come up
Empty and dip again and again.

Flight

Zagreb, 1919

In this story my grandmother tells
Three women thrash wheat
On a circle of stone.
They make good gossip as they work
And the youngest daughter
Hears the drone before she sees
The dark shape eating air.
They all watch the sky,
They shade their eyes,
But like a long moment of work
Forgotten, sung through,
The biplane passes
And they bolt through the wheat
To the house of their father
Who hears her scream before he sees
Her arms in the air as wings—
The youngest girl
Outdistancing her sisters, her skirts
Pulled up around her thighs.
He takes her in the rough pasture
Into his arms to listen
To the huge bird, the flight, the shadow
Burned into wheat.

Burning Shit at An Khe

Into that pit
   I had to climb down
With a rake and matches; eventually,
   You had to do something
Because it just kept piling up
   And it wasn't our country, it wasn't
Our air thick with the sick smoke
   So another soldier and I
Lifted the shelter off its blocks
   To expose the home-made toilets:
Fifty-five gallon drums cut in half
   With crude wood seats that splintered.
We soaked the piles in fuel oil
   And lit the stuff
And tried to keep the fire burning.
   To take my first turn
I paid some kid
   A care package of booze from home.
I'd walked past the burning once
   And gagged the whole heart of myself—
It smelled like the world
   Was on fire,
But when my turn came again
   There was no one
So I stuffed cotton up my nose
   And marched up that hill. We poured
And poured until it burned and black
   Smoke curdled
But the fire went out.
   Heavy artillery

Hammered the evening away in the distance,
  Vietnamese laundry women watched
From a safe place, laughing.
  I'd grunted out eight months
Of jungle and thought I had a grip on things
  But we flipped the coin and I lost
And climbed down into my fellow soldiers'
  Shit and began to sink and didn't stop
Until I was deep to my knees. Liftships
  Cut the air above me, the hacking
Blast of their blades
  Ripped dust in swirls so every time
I tried to light a match
  It died
And it all came down on me, the stink
  And the heat and the worthlessness
Until I slipped and climbed
  Out of that hole and ran
Past the olive drab
  Tents and trucks and clothes and everything
Green as far from the shit
  As the fading light allowed.
Only now I can't fly.
  I lay down in it
And finger paint the words of who I am
  Across my chest
Until I'm covered and there's only one smell,
  One word.

1955

After mass father rinsed the chalice with wine
Again and again.
Drunk before noon
He'd sleep it off in the sacristy
While the other altar boys and I
Rummaged through the sacred things, feeling up
The blessed linen and silk vestments,
Swinging the censer above us so it whistled.
We put our hands on everything we could reach
Then woke the father for mass.

In summer the wool cassock itched
And I sweated through the white lace surplice.
My head reeled from incense
So I mumbled through the Latin prayers
And learned to balance the paten
Gracefully under their chins, my face
Turned away from the priest
Who dipped into the cup
As if to pluck a fish
And just like that something took me by the brain
And I saw myself
Torn loose from the congregation,

Floating like an impossible
Balloon of myself and I thought
This must be what my life is
Though I didn't know what it meant
And I couldn't move or swallow and thought I'd panic
Until father scowled and nudged me down the altar railing
To the next mouth

Open in the O of acceptance
So much like a scream
That can't get out of the lungs . . .
I don't know why my hands should shake,
I'm only remembering something.

Song for the Lost Private

The night we were to meet in the hotel
In the forbidden Cholon district
You didn't show
So I drank myself into a filthy room with a bar girl
Who had terrible scars
She ran her fingers over
As we bartered for the night.
Drunk I couldn't do anything, angry
I threw the mattress to the street
And stood out on the balcony naked,
Cursing your name to the night.
She thought I was crazy,
She tried to give my money back.
I don't know how to say I tried again.
I saw myself in the mirror and couldn't move.
In her fist she crushed the paper money,
She curled in sleep away from me
So I felt cruel, cold, and small arms fire
Cracked in the marketplace below.
I thought I heard you call back my name then
But white flares lit the sky
Casting empty streets in clean light
And the firing stopped.
I couldn't sleep so I touched her
Small shoulders, traced the curve of her spine,
Traced the scars, the miles
We were all from home.

Killing Chickens

Never mind what you think,
The old man did not rush
Recklessly into the coop the last minute.
The chickens hardly stirred
For the easy way he sang to them.
Red sun is burning out
Past slag heaps of the mill. The old man
Touches the blade of his killing knife
With his fat thumb.
I'm in the backyard on a quilt
Spread out under the heavy dark plums
He cooks for his whiskey.
He walks among the hens singing
His chicken song way down in his throat
Until he finds the one who's ready
And he holds her to his barrel chest.

What did you think?
Did you think you just jerk the bird
From her roost and hack her head off?

Beyond the coop
I see the fleeting white dress of my grandmother
As she crosses and recrosses the porch
To fill the bucket with scalding water.
How easy the feathers will come
When she drowns them for plucking
And clouds the air with a stench
I can't stand not to breathe.
I'm not even a boy yet but I watch
The old man sing out into the yard,

His knife already at the chicken's throat
When everything begins to spin in my world—
He slices off the head without a squawk
And swirls the bird in circles, a fine
Blood spray fanning out far enough
To reach me where I wait
Obediently, where I can't stop watching
The head the old man picks up,
His free hand become a puppet chicken
Clucking at me, pecking my head with the cold beak
Until I cry for him to stop
Until he pins me down, clucking, laughing, blood
All over his hands.

He did it so I would remember him
I tell myself all these years later.
He did it because it was his last summer
Among us. In August he didn't feel the fly
Come into his cancerous ear and lay its eggs.
He didn't feel the maggots hatch
As he sat dazed with pills in the sun.
He pecked my head and laughed out of love,
Out of love he snatched me roughly to his chest
And sang his foreign songs way,
Way down in his throat.

Dream of Santiago, 1973

The stadium's full of undressed men
Who draw their arms and legs up into themselves
As if tucked wings could allow their disappearance
Across the soccer field
Cast wildly with their shadows.
All the nameless
Herded in the dark.
All the children chased through narrow streets
Want to rise away from soldiers
Who drag them down.

I wake sweating, at attention
To keep myself from falling to the streets.
You sleep so hard in your crib
You don't wake when I brush back hair
Roughly from your eyes.
Through the bedroom's dirty window
Light slashes and I imagine
The children have come
For food that no one's thought to bring,

But it's only a flock of birds
Rattling their wings,
Only the winter-ragged starlings
Come again to haggle over stale bread
Some old woman in the street
Scatters from her porch.

The Last Lie

Some guy in the miserable convoy
Raised up in the back of our open truck
And threw a can of c-rations at a child
Who called into the rumble for food.
He didn't toss the can, he wound up and hung it
On the child's forehead and she was stunned
Backwards into the dust of our trucks.

Across the sudden angle of the road's curving
I could still see her when she rose
Waving one hand across her swollen, bleeding head,
Wildly swinging her other hand
At the children who mobbed her,
Who tried to take her food.

I grit my teeth to myself to remember that girl
Smiling as she fought off her brothers and sisters.
She laughed
As if she thought it were a joke
And the guy with me laughed
And fingered the edge of another can
Like it was the seam of a baseball
Until his rage ripped
Again into the faces of children
Who called to us for food.

Hope

Joe works in the pipe mill and he's proud
Of his job, of how lazy he can be
Once the day's work is done;
How he can sleep between machines
Or in the huge pyramids of pipe.
His knuckles are torn.
He drinks too much and hates
Anybody who is not white.
He married a woman who never left her home town,
Who stayed near the mother
She fights on the phone every day.

They have two small boys and Joe loves them
So fiercely it's frightening.
Joe says he'd kill for them and he smiles
So you wonder why he thinks this,
What kind of terror he must imagine
To think he'd ever have to kill for his children.

His days are so often our nights
And his nights our days he seems
A zombie between shifts,
Out of sync with the rest of us.
He can be edgy on these days, wild,
Slamming his fists at walls
Or lashing the air with a bottle of beer.
Other times he can be so tender,
As with his children in the evening
Curled up in his lap, scrubbed, whispering
Their battle against sleep, and once,

I watched him lift a dog from the highway.
Howling, its hind legs crushed,

The dog tried to reach around and bite Joe
As he carried it, dodging traffic,
To the soft grass of the shoulder.
I waited in the car and watched.
Stunned by what he'd done
Joe stumbled in the headlight spears
Of cars tearing past too close.
He'd saved a thing from dying as far as he could
And now he was lost.
He shook his fist at the traffic
And when I opened the door
He screamed to get back in
And he reached down and strangled that dog.

What are you going to do he said,
That dog didn't have no hope
And we drove out of our way
To pass close to the mill . . . Night
So you could see the gas flame up
Blue and white from the low stacks of the open hearth.
He breathed deeply and slowed the car to a cruise
As if the slag air revived him,
As if the flaming steel and shitty bars
And the steady grind of a mile of industry
Were blood in his heart
And his heart needed blood.

The Ghost Inside

1

Like Ezekiel
Unless the ghost is inside you
Your tongue is tied
And your hands with which you otherwise gesture,
Twisting in the air before you will not move,
Nor your arms, your legs,
And in your eyes you look a hundred years old.

2

It is so long now
The bodies have grown back into the earth,
Into the green places, the shadowy
Plantations abandoned by white egrets
Who will not return
To the war-fouled groves of bamboo,
But the cocaine is even whiter,
Spread out on the mirror
Into which you make your grotesque faces,

Whiter than this sky full of holes
Opening like flowers into the humorless oblivion beyond.
Unless the ghost is upon you
You can't speak a word
And tonight a razor of ice slides through your brain.
You lie back on the stoop and hear the evening
Of birdsong rise and fall
And only a few black wings roll past.

Temple near Quang Tri, Not on the Map

Dusk, the ivy thick with sparrows
Squawking for more room
Is all we hear; we see
Birds move on the walls of the temple
Shaping their calligraphy of wings.
Ivy is thick in the grottos,
On the moon-watching platform
And ivy keeps the door from fully closing.

The point man leads us and we are
Inside, lifting
The white washbowl, the smaller bowl
For rice, the stone lanterns
And carved stone heads that open
Above the carved faces for incense.
But even the bamboo sleeping mat
Rolled in the corner,
Even the place of prayer is clean.
And a small man

Sits legs askew in the shadow
The farthest wall casts
Halfway across the room.
He is bent over, his head
Rests on the floor and he is speaking something
As though to us and not to us.
The CO wants to ignore him;
He locks and loads and fires a clip into the walls
Which are not packed with rice this time
And tells us to move out.

But one of us moves towards the man,
Curious about what he is saying.

We bend him to sit straight
And when he's nearly peaked
At the top of his slow uncurling
His face becomes visible, his eyes
Roll down to the charge
Wired between his teeth and the floor.
The sparrows
Burst off the walls into the jungle.

Weeds Among the Garlic

I could lie here all day
Under the sagging plum tree branches
Watching the bent old woman
Weed her patch of garlic
So patiently and so carefully
She looks as though she were raising someone
From the dead.

Only once all afternoon has she paused
To drink from a sweaty glass of water
She keeps cupped
In the loose dirt at her feet.
She brushed at webs of hair then
With the backs of her hands,
Her fingers all painted red dirt,
Her fine hair
Pulling out from under the babushka.

She's brought with her to our lives
The blood and thick skin
Of an old country
Slowly burning out in her brain. This evening,
Starlings begin to gather
And the different tunes of locust
Start up high in the broken oaks
And the fathers come home at last for supper
So it almost seems possible to live
Among the shit and lies
That haunt the life outside this moment.

I need her to stay there,
Forever pulling the thin green

Leaves of weeds from among her garlic
Because with her love
She keeps me from spinning off the earth,
At bay she keeps black clouds
That gather behind my eyes,
That look as though
Fingers had torn them apart.

Surrounding Blues on the Way Down

I was barely in country.
We slipped under rain black clouds
Opening around us like orchids.
He'd come to take me into the jungle
So I felt the loneliness
Though I did not yet hate the beautiful war.
Eighteen years old and a man
Was telling me how to stay alive
In the tropics he said would rot me—

Brothers of the heart he said and smiled
Until we came upon a mama san
Bent over from her stuffed sack of flowers.
We flew past her but he hit the brakes hard,
He spun the tires backwards in the mud.
He did not hate the war either,
Other reasons made him cry out to her
So she stopped,
She smiled her beetle black teeth at us.
In the air she raised her arms.

I have no excuse for myself.
I sat in that man's jeep in the rain
And watched him slam her to her knees,
The plastic butt of his M-16
Crashing down on her.
I was barely in country, the clouds
Hung like huge flowers, black
Like her teeth.

Hotel Florence

The woman finished her song,
Drank herself drunk and drove alone all night.
Waiting for her
I read the paper in the rococo lobby,
Nothing to say to anyone.
Later, sun already up in the dirty sky
She came in her solitude.
I half-dozed, half-dreamed like a shadow
Across the bed
When she stepped out of the lit bathroom
Like a small boy in her white pajamas, her rings
And necklaces cupped in her hands before her.
We whispered face to face
In the room of strangers,
We tried to name the thing we were together,
The Texas dawn grinding . . .

Or I can say no.
Say the bed is empty and I'm alone
And years pass and miles,
Miles come between.
It does no good to shake your head for answers,
There are only the hard lessons you must pay,
Only the sharp wings of being alive
That beat inside.

Letter to X.

There's much I haven't told you.
I closed my eyes and saw you
As a boy in Berlin
Only moments after the war
Had finally murdered itself out
In the streets and in the hidden
Bunkers of the privileged and the insane.
You're on your bicycle, neat with your books
And your thin suit,
And you've paused, one foot on the pedal,
One foot in the grave debris
Of the dead city
As if something out of the frame of memory
Has caught your eye.

Behind you fires burn.
The clock in the tower in the center
Of the square is stuck.
Women in the streets
Stooped under their babushkas
Bear crosses of light,
And their men
Hide in dark coats.
They are as ghosts and the world has stopped
Turning and is pitching
Through blue space.
I write this on the afternoon the budded trees have frozen.
Our breath makes it hard for us to see
The faces in this cold.

Elegy for A.

Four years since the morning you leaped
Out from under the waves of pain
Into which you had to awake
One day in the middle of your life.
I think of you
Nights my own confusion
Runs away with itself,
Darting in and out of the dark
Possibilities like a spirit.
I don't know if I can speak to you,
I don't know why we long so for the dead
Who can do us no good, eventually,
Like you, a flood of stars will drown us all.

You jumped because at three A.M.
You passed the open balcony door
And for the hundredth night you couldn't sleep.
That day in your bed I'd tried to hold you,
To drag you back to us
But I didn't understand the way you
Floundered with your arms,
The way you gulped for air.
Inside you something was shaking out of control,
Something was wrong.

Four years already.
I wanted to tell you that my son
Who bears your name into the world
Is strong and sure of himself;
That your wife has found someone else, someone
Remarkably like you

In your gentle time,
And that sometimes, friend, I close my eyes
To see you descend on the wings of your bathrobe,
Speaking, I imagine, some warning in the instant it took
Before you smashed away
The hold the dark had on you.

Sun

Neon sun dead over us
We picnic near the river.
We have come so far from the everlasting
Traffic, through corn rows, through woods
And across fields we may never
Find our way back home; one lonely farmer
Mows the thick grass
Back and forth across our vision.
We have come so far from our decision

To park the car and walk into the high
Time of an afternoon we stole.
Come close and let me see you inches
From my face as vision blurs then clears again.
I want to trace the lines and wrinkles,
I want to mend
The scars while we have time and care
Enough to break the rope, the selfishness
That binds. Long
May this light blast down on us.

On the Wing

The pond the trees and the burning
Field of poppies
Stop turning when the wind stops.
I waded
Down the length of the old man's pond
So I could watch the heron
Stalk the bank for frogs.

Because he listened for me in the grass
I could walk to the light
Chop of surface
Cut by the wind that cold morning.

I was that near him when he rose
So easily I felt the breath of something—
Crest or wing or translucent feet—
Pass my face.

Well, if that's what I am, home
With my shoes filled with mud
And the dust of wings still
Burning my face
Then the touch of a white thing
Flying over and away from me
Is everything,
Day in, day out,
When the sky is absolutely white
And we are on the wing.

Noise

Next door the newlyweds
Scream at each other, three A.M.
I hate your fucking guts he says
Through the open summer window
To the sky crowded with stars.
Freight trains at the roundhouse
Shake the windows, shake the house.
Just please get out she says
And someone throws something
Glass against the wall.
This is none of my business
But they've waked me with their noise.
The clots of stars or the full moon
Could be behind this because I feel the same
Anger and the trains make so much noise tonight.

Everyone lies and cheats and says hateful things.
The newlyweds next door
Spit the words out at each other.
From room to room I see them move
In their underwear, the windows
Open, she is lovely, she is
Wringing her hands
And he is pacing in another room then disappears
And she is standing by the window, crying,
The trains so loud tonight
And the trainmen shout the couplings into place—
A triangle of nervous noise
Because the noise is in my head too,
The noise is always in my head.

Regret for the Mourning Doves
Who Failed to Mate

I passed the window and saw their lovely flash of wings
In the ivy all tangled and fluttering.
Something about gravity is deeply important
To whether or not it works for them
And gravity keeps these two from mating.
Even in the rain he tried
His small dance up her back
As she clung to the ivy
Easing the angle for him.
But I'm sorry,

I'm here to say they didn't make it.
Their nest stays empty
And the wind eats it up bit by bit
The way they constructed it together—
Some twigs, some brown grass woven,
A bit of color from a scrap of paper
Returned to litter the street.
And the winter keeps us locked indoors
Where we peck at each other,
Our voices thin and cold
Saying always what we don't mean,
Our hearts all future,
Our love nearly gone.

Mercy

Enough snow over last night's ice
So the road appears safe, appears
As a long white scar unfolding.
Ohio, cold hawk off Lake Erie,
And only enough light to see vague outlines:
The castle-like shape of mill stacks
And the shape of gulls' wings
Dipping to the parking lot for garbage
Lashed this way and that by the wind
These nights have in common.
I pumped gas from five to midnight
For minimum wage
Because I had a family and the war
Made me stupid, and only dead enough
To clean windshields.
When you clean the windshields of others
You see your own face
Reflected in the glass.
I looked and saw only enough hope
To lift me car to car and in between
I breathed the oil smell and the fly strips
And the vending candy air.
The *Gulf* sign clanged in the gale,
The plate glass strained like a voice
I thought would shatter
Yet still cars arrived, dim headlights
Casting the snow into a silver sheet,
Then the fenders like low clouds,
Then the bundled families
And the hushed sound

When father opens the window
And slips me the money for gas.
Only a second when our eyes catch
And the wind shows some mercy.

For the Wife Beater's Wife

With blue irises her face is blossomed. Blue
Circling to yellow, circling to brown on her cheeks.
The long bone of her jaw untracked
She hides in our kitchen.
He sleeps it off next door.

Her chicken legs tucked under her
She's frantic with lies, animated
Before the swirling smoke.
On her cigarette she leaves red prints, red
Like a cut on the white cup.
Like a skin she pulls her sweater around her.
She's cold,
She brings the cold in with her.

In our kitchen she hides.
He sleeps it off next door, his great
Belly heaving with booze.
Again and again she tells the story
As if the details ever changed,
As if blows to the face were somehow
Different beating to beating.

We reach for her but can't help.
She retreats into her cold love of him
And looks across the table at us
As if across a sea.
Next door he claws out of sleep.
She says she thinks she'll do something
After all, with her hair tonight.

Vaudeville

At the Pearl Street gate to the steel mill
In Fatty's Bar and Grille
A man and his monkey
Dressed like twins slipped in.

I have seen turtles suck up
Beer from an ashtray on the bar.
I have heard dogs seem to say
I love you,
The sound like the rasp of Isaiah,
Hot coals on his tongue—
We read the lips and we believe.

But this monkey took a long drink and looked over at me
Rolling back his eyes
As if remembering another place
And the air around me seemed a membrane
Enfolding the sensible world
And something came from inside me
To hug the body so terribly like mine,
The monkey, no myth this time,
Grinning, howling, never letting go.

Small Song for Andrew

My baby boy cries and cries and cries
So we feed him and love him
And walk into the cool autumn night
Traffic streaking past
We play music for him
Dance him around the house
Pull out bowls and lids and spoons
Dial the phone so he can hear
Love long distance
Ride him in the stroller
Kiss his face and neck and feet
We rock him
We sing to him
Until finally he sleeps
So deeply he hangs his head
Backwards into my arms
So I carry him into his warm room
And its jungle of our indulgences
And he is more beautiful
Than the light
Before the light has touched anything

Homage to Elvis, Homage to the Fathers

All night the pimps' cars slide past the burning mill
Where I've come back
To breathe the slag stink air of home.
Without words the gray workers trade shifts,
The serious drinkers fill the bar
To dull the steel ringing their brains.

As I remember, as I want it to be,
The Buicks are pastel, pale
In the light burning out
Of the city's dirty side
Where we lived out our life
Sentences in a company house,
Good people to love and fight, matters
Of the lucky heart that doesn't stop.

Beyond the mill street
Slag heaps loom up like dunes, almost beautiful.
Once we played our war games there
And a boy from the block ran screaming
He's here, it's him at the record store
And we slid down the sooty waste of the mill
And black and grimy we stood outside
Behind our screaming older sisters
And saw him, his hair puffed up and shiny, his gold
Bracelets catching light.

He changed us somehow: we cleaned up,
We spun the 45s in the basement,
Danced on the cool concrete and plastered
Our hair back like his and twisted

Our forbidden hips.
Across the alley our fathers died
Piece by piece among the blast furnace rumble.
They breathed the steel rifted air
As if it were good.

Unwelcome, I stand outside the mill gates,
Watch workers pass as ghosts.
I close my eyes and it all makes sense.
I believe I will live forever.
I believe the world will rip apart
From the inside
Of our next moment alive.

The Streets

On this day in this year of strangeness
The starlings may or may not
Come and I stay too long at the window
Waiting for the oily rainbow wings,
For the feet that are crosses in the snow.
In this long rift of speechlessness
I fall away from my life
And the cold careless winter. Fall

Through dark space to surface
In the river where we swam as children,
My arms treading water, rippling circles,
The locust clacking,
All the days of a life left,
All the hate buried deep another season.

Yet what I love is close at hand:
Wind cutting through the city
Street after mad street;
Circle of starlings when they come
Like blossoms in the waking landscape of a city
Where the gentle die,
Where the bad go on pounding the air.

The Artificial Waterfall
and Woods Scene Clock

The artificial waterfall and woods scene clock you bought
Doesn't tick or tock, it
Grinds the time away.
You love to turn the bulb inside on,
To watch the blue water
Glisten in your dark room,
The rocks blaze up.

Rain again. Rain
General on the coast tonight
And so early in spring for such storms. Yesterday
The sky was the yellow of the sick and dying,
The air like cotton
We tried to touch through
But couldn't feel enough of anything
To shake this nagging uneasy tow of time.

In the dark your knitting needles click
And I watch for signs of your own death shroud
Unfolding from the huge balls of yarn at your feet.
Already you've abandoned the gaudy
Colors of comforters
And favor the earth's browns and grays,
The browns and grays of the waterfall
And woods scene clock.

Snowy Egret

My neighbor's boy has lifted his father's shotgun and stolen
Down to the backwaters of the Elizabeth
And in the moon he's blasted a snowy egret
From the shallows it stalked for small fish.

Midnight. My wife wakes me. He's in the backyard
With a shovel so I go down half-drunk with pills
That let me sleep to see what I can see and if it's safe.
The boy doesn't hear me come across the dewy grass.
He says through tears he has to bury it,
He says his father will kill him
And he digs until the hole is deep enough and gathers
The egret carefully into his arms
As if not to harm the blood-splattered wings
Gleaming in the flashlight beam.

His man's muscled shoulders
Shake with the weight of what he can't set right no matter
    what,
But one last time he tries to stay a child, sobbing
Please don't tell . . .
He says he only meant to flush it from the shadows,
He only meant to watch it fly
But the shot spread too far
Ripping into the white wings
Spanned awkwardly for a moment
Until it glided into brackish death.

I want to grab his shoulders,
Shake the lies loose from his lips but he hurts enough,
He burns with shame for what he's done,

With fear for his hard father's
Fists I've seen crash down on him for so much less.
I don't know what to do but hold him.
If I let go he'll fly to pieces before me.
What a time we share, that can make a good boy steal away,
Wiping out from the blue face of the pond
What he hadn't even known he loved, blasting
Such beauty into nothing.

Song of Napalm

for my wife

After the storm, after the rain stopped pounding,
We stood in the doorway watching horses
Walk off lazily across the pasture's hill.
We stared through the black screen,
Our vision altered by the distance
So I thought I saw a mist
Kicked up around their hooves when they faded
Like cut-out horses
Away from us.
The grass was never more blue in that light, more
Scarlet; beyond the pasture
Trees scraped their voices into the wind, branches
Criss-crossed the sky like barbed wire
But you said they were only branches.

Okay. The storm stopped pounding.
I am trying to say this straight: for once
I was sane enough to pause and breathe
Outside my wild plans and after the hard rain
I turned my back on the old curses. I believed
They swung finally away from me . . .

But still the branches are wire
And thunder is the pounding mortar,
Still I close my eyes and see the girl
Running from her village, napalm
Stuck to her dress like jelly,

Her hands reaching for the no one
Who waits in waves of heat before her.

So I can keep on living,
So I can stay here beside you,
I try to imagine she runs down the road and wings
Beat inside her until she rises
Above the stinking jungle and her pain
Eases, and your pain, and mine.

But the lie swings back again.
The lie works only as long as it takes to speak
And the girl runs only as far
As the napalm allows
Until her burning tendons and crackling
Muscles draw her up
Into that final position
Burning bodies so perfectly assume. Nothing
Can change that; she is burned behind my eyes
And not your good love and not the rain-swept air
And not the jungle green
Pasture unfolding before us can deny it.

Other Titles in the Contemporary Poetry Series